THE GREEKS

ARE COMING!

Paul Mason

Illustrated by Martin Bustamante

W
FRANKLIN WATTS
LONDON•SYDNEY

Franklin Watts
Published in paperback in Great Britain in 2020 by
The Watts Publishing Group
Copyright © The Watts Publishing
Group 2018

Credits
Series Editor: Julia Bird
Illustrator: Martin Bustamante
Packaged by: Collaborate Agency

ISBN 978 1 4451 5689 7

Image Credits
p.2 tl: © Pecold/Shutterstock.com. p.3 br: © Pecold/Shutterstock.com. p. 4 br : ©
Constantinos Iliopoulos/Shutterstock Every.com. p.5 tr: © Mati Nitibhon/Shutterstock.com.
p.5 bl: © Pecold/Shutterstock.com. p.7 br: © Renata Sedmakova/Shutterstock.com. p.9 br:
© krechet/Shutterstock.com. p.11 bl: © Gilmanshin/Shutterstock.com. p.11 bl: © Dario Lo
Presti/Shutterstock.com. p.13 br: © Zoran Karapancev/Shutterstock.com. p.15 tr: © Kostas
Koutsaftikis/Shutterstock.com. p.17 cr: Stéphane Magnenat/© Wikimedia Commons. p.19
bc: © Mark Higgins/Shutterstock.com. p.21 tr: © Ulmus Media/Shutterstock.com. p.23 bc ©
Meinzahn.Istock. p.25 br : © Jan Willem van Hofwegen/Shutterstock.com. p.27 br: © Haris
Vythoulkas / Shutterstock.com. p.28 tr: © Haris Vythoulkas/Shutterstock.com. p.28 br: ©
Anastasios71/Shutterstock.com. p.29 bl: © Lazyllama/Shutterstock.com

Franklin Watts
An imprint of
Hachette Children's Group
Part of The Watts Publishing Group
Carmelite House
50 Victoria Embankment
London EC4Y 0DZ

An Hachette UK Company
www.hachette.co.uk
www.franklinwatts.co.uk

Printed in Dubai

CONTENTS

The Ancient Greek world   4

The Greeks are coming!   6

The Spartans   8

Greek hoplites   10

Archers and cavalry   12

The Battle of Marathon   14

The defence of Athens   16

Thanks to Athena   18

The Greek navy   20

Greek settlers   22

Greek entertainment   24

Crime and punishment   26

The rise and fall of Ancient Greece   28

Glossary   30

Great Greek insults   30

Finding out more   31

Index   32

Words in **bold** are
in the glossary
on page 30.

THE ANCIENT GREEK WORLD

Today, Greece is a country with **borders** you can see on a map. Ancient Greece was not like this. Its territory was divided among lots of powerful city-states and islands.

Hellas

Ancient Greece was known as Hellas, and its people called themselves Hellenes. 'Greeks' is a name they were given later, by the Romans. The Greek city-states sometimes fought each other and sometimes made **alliances**. But they usually joined together to defend Greece from attacks by its great **rivals**, the Carthaginians and the Persians.

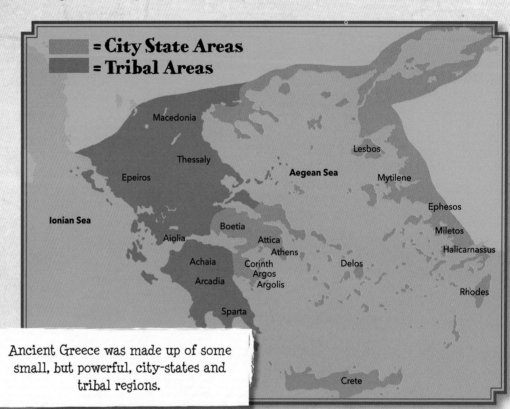

= City State Areas
= Tribal Areas

Macedonia

Thessaly

Epeiros

Lesbos

Aegean Sea

Mytilene

Ionian Sea

Ephesos

Boetia

Miletos

Aiolia

Attica

Athens

Halicarnassus

Achaia

Corinth
Argos

Delos

Arcadia

Argolis

Rhodes

Sparta

Crete

Ancient Greece was made up of some small, but powerful, city-states and tribal regions.

Greek civilisations

Between about 2200 BCE and 30 BCE, ancient Greece produced some powerful civilisations:

2200-1450 BCE: Minoans

On the island of Crete, the Minoans built great palaces and produced high-quality pottery, jewellery, statues and carvings. Minoan ships traded across the eastern Mediterranean.

The ruins of the ancient Palace of Knossos on Crete. The palace was the centre of the Minoan civilisation.

1450-1100 BCE: Mycenaeans

The Mycenaeans came from Mycenae in mainland Greece. They were great builders and warriors. Their most famous war was against the city of Troy. Legend says the Mycenaeans got into Troy by hiding inside a wooden horse. In about 1100 BCE, the Mycenaean civilisation collapsed. No one is really sure why.

A model of the famous wooden horse of Troy. The horse appears in a famous epic poem called the *Odyssey*, by the ancient Greek writer Homer.

Out of the dark

Between 1100 and 800 BCE, Greece entered the Dark Age, a time we know very little about. Afterwards, Greek city-states started to become increasingly powerful. They began to build great temples, make scientific discoveries and fight wars for power and territory. Greece's growth brought it into conflict with the mighty Persian Empire, to the east. By 490 BCE, the Persians had decided to teach the Greeks a lesson ...

HOW DO WE KNOW?

We get evidence about life in ancient Greece from a variety of **sources**. The Greeks left behind lots of writing, ranging from plays to carvings on tombs, which tells us about their world.

We can also investigate **archaeological** evidence from ancient Greece. Buildings, jewellery, cooking equipment and weapons from the time have survived for thousands of years.

In ancient Greece, laurel wreaths were given to the winners of competitions. They wore them on their heads like crowns. A golden wreath like this one would have been awarded for an important victory.

THE GREEKS ARE COMING!

If anyone ever tells you they don't get nervous before a big battle, they're lying. Every one of us Persian soldiers has a stomach fluttering like there's a swarm of bees buzzing inside it!

TROUBLESOME GREEKS

We Persians are looking forward to giving the Greeks of Athens a good hiding. They only have themselves to blame. They started it!

The Athenians have been trying to chip away at our power for years. Nine years ago, they helped people in Ionia to **revolt** against us. The Ionian Revolt got worse and worse. A year after it had begun, the Athenians and Ionians **sacked** our city of Sardis. Our king, Darius, was absolutely furious! He went around swearing revenge on the Greeks. He told a servant that he had to say to Darius three times every day:

'Master, remember the Athenians.'

It was a reminder that they had to be dealt with.

TAKING BACK CONTROL

It took four years for the Ionian Revolt to be crushed. We finally got things under control and got rid of the Athenians two years ago. Now, here we are – a Persian army of over 20,000 men, camped out not far from Athens, at a little place called Marathon.

READY FOR REVENGE

The Greeks will have to try to defend Athens. Otherwise we will burn their city to the ground, just as they did Sardis. We know the Greeks are coming our way. Finally, it looks like Darius (and the rest of Persia) will get their revenge!

HOW DO WE KNOW?

One source of information about the Ionian Revolt is a book called the *Histories*. It is about the wars between the Greeks and the Persians. The *Histories* was written in about 425 BCE by a man named Herodotus (c. 485–420 BCE). He is often described as the first modern historian.

Herodotus was not completely **neutral** about the Persians. Not only was he Greek, but his family had been **exiled** from its original home by a Persian overlord.

A statue of the famous historian Herodotus

THE SPARTANS

One thing the Persian army is very happy about is that there are no Greeks from Sparta anywhere around. Fighting Spartans is nobody's idea of a good time.

BORN WARRIORS

Sparta must be the most war-like part of Greece. Spartan men are trained as warriors virtually from birth. Boys leave home at seven years old to start their military training. For the next TWENTY-THREE years they practise to become fully fledged warriors. Only those who make it through are considered true Spartans. As a result, the Spartan army is extremely tough.

HELP FROM SPARTA?

When Athens is threatened from outside, you would normally expect Sparta to come to help fight off the invader. Fortunately, though, the Spartans are busy with their biggest religious festival, Carneia. Their army never leaves Sparta during Carneia.

King Darius and his generals knew all this when they planned our attack, of course. It will be days before the festival ends and the Spartans can send help. Long before the help arrives, Athens will have burned to the ground.

HOW DO WE KNOW?

We know about the Persian invasion of Greece not only from written sources such as Herodotus (see page 7), but also from archaeology.

At Marathon there is a large burial ground for the dead, giving an idea of how many soldiers died. And weapons, such as arrowheads from the feared Persian archers or the remains of Greek **javelins,** tell us more about how the battle was fought.

This temple was built after the clash between the Persians and the Greeks at Marathon, partly to honour those Greeks who died in the fighting.

OUTNUMBERED GREEKS

We have another reason to feel confident that victory will be ours – there are a lot more Persian soldiers than Greek ones. Word is, the Athenians have about 9,000 of their own troops, plus 1,000 of their allies, the Plataeans. But there are over 20,000 Persian troops eagerly awaiting the battle.

GREEK HOPLITES

Lots of us have fought against the Greek hoplites before, in Ionia. Even though we outnumber them at least two to one, we know this battle will not be easy.

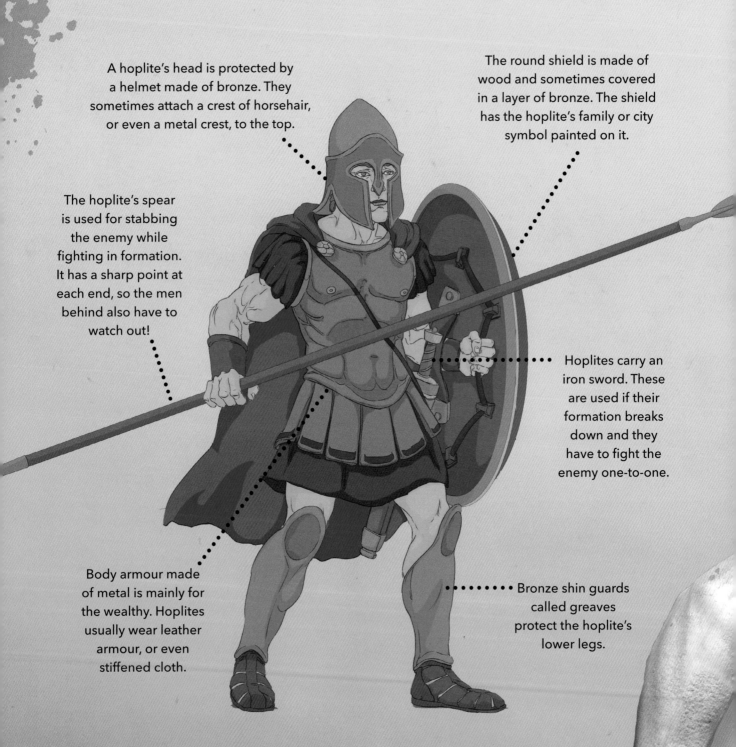

A hoplite's head is protected by a helmet made of bronze. They sometimes attach a crest of horsehair, or even a metal crest, to the top.

The round shield is made of wood and sometimes covered in a layer of bronze. The shield has the hoplite's family or city symbol painted on it.

The hoplite's spear is used for stabbing the enemy while fighting in formation. It has a sharp point at each end, so the men behind also have to watch out!

Hoplites carry an iron sword. These are used if their formation breaks down and they have to fight the enemy one-to-one.

Body armour made of metal is mainly for the wealthy. Hoplites usually wear leather armour, or even stiffened cloth.

Bronze shin guards called greaves protect the hoplite's lower legs.

FIERCE PHALANX

The hoplites fight as a team. They line up side-by-side and lock their shields together. They make eight or ten lines like this, one behind the other. Their long spears bristle at you like porcupine quills over the tops of the shields. The Greeks call these formations phalanxes.

Once a phalanx starts moving towards you, it is hard to stop. The Persian archers will rain down arrows on them, but if the hoplites get within spear-stabbing range, we'll be in trouble.

HOW DO WE KNOW?

The Greeks left behind many images of their hoplites in art and on pottery.

We know from archaeological discoveries that most of these images are accurate. Helmets, spearheads, armour and other metal items have all survived from the time of the ancient Greeks. They show us how the Greek hoplites fought and the weapons they used.

Ancient Greek war helmets were designed to cover and protect as much of the face as possible.

ARCHERS AND CAVALRY

Hoplites are not the only fighters in a Greek army. The Greeks also use archers and **cavalry** – though not in the same way as Persians.

FLYING ARROWS

We Persians bring many archers to a battle – they are one of our main weapons. Our archers shelter behind wicker screens and let fly with **volley** after volley of arrows. Although the arrows do not fly a long way, they do stop enemy soldiers or cavalry before they can reach us.

The Greeks never have as many archers as we do. In fact, they sometimes do not have any at all – and every Persian soldier is hoping that's the case at Marathon. Athenian archers are mostly **mercenaries** from elsewhere. They hide in the phalanxes, sheltered behind shields. Instead of firing volleys, they usually take aim at individual targets.

ON HORSEBACK

The Greeks do use cavalry – troops that fight from horseback. As with archers, though, they do not use cavalry as much as we do. In fact, our spies tell us they may not have any cavalry at all for this battle.

To a Persian soldier, that's unbelievable: cavalry and archers are the two most important forces in our army. We cannot imagine winning a battle without them. For the Greeks, though, the hoplites come first, then everything else.

HOW DO WE KNOW?

The Persian tactic of using archers to fire volleys of arrows is described by Herodotus. He reported that:

'When they fired their bows, they hid the Sun with the mass of arrows.'

Herodotus also told how the education of Persian boys showed how important archery was in Persia:

'[They] are educated from the time they are five years old until they are twenty, but they study only three things: horsemanship, archery and honesty.'

A frieze of Persian archers that dates from the 5th century BCE. They used a bow made of horn and wood, bound together using resin.

THE BATTLE OF MARATHON

The Battle at Marathon is over. What's left of the Persian army – including me, thank **Mithra** – is back aboard our ships. What a disaster! Instead of a great Persian victory, the Athenians beat us soundly.

TAKEN BY SURPRISE

The battle began when the Greeks launched a sudden attack. It was madness! We outnumbered them, and we realised later that it was true they had no archers and no cavalry. But they formed into phalanxes anyway, and came at us.

Our archers tried valiantly to stop the hoplites, but their arrows were not heavy enough to get through the Greek shields and armour. They could only stop the Greeks by landing arrows directly on their bodies – and not always then. Before we knew it, the Greeks were upon us.

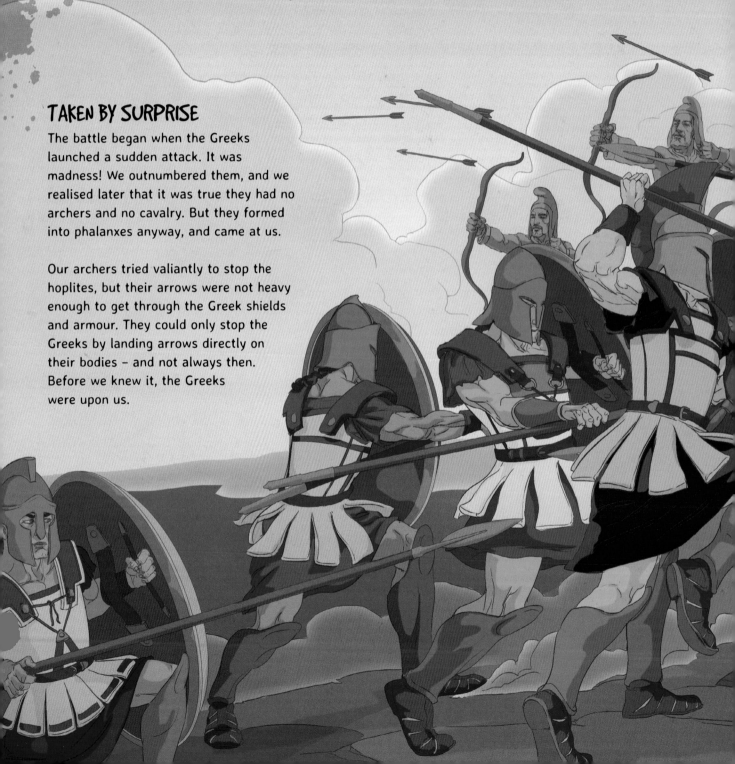

A CUNNING PLAN

Now that the battle is over, our generals understand just how clever the Greek **strategy** was. Their general, Miltiades, had fought in the Persian army years ago. He knew that our strongest soldiers always go in the middle of our line. Miltiades put his strongest hoplites at the ends.

Our soldiers in the middle broke through the Greek line. Our troops on either side, though, fled from the strong hoplite forces attacking them. The Persians in the middle suddenly had Greek hoplites on three sides. They were practically surrounded, and most were massacred before they could get back to our ships.

Six thousand men – over a quarter of our army – is gone. Only a few hundred Greeks seem to have been killed.

Aeschylus (c.525-456 BCE), the Greek poet and playwright who fought for Athens at the Battle of Marathon.

HOW DO WE KNOW?

The victory at Marathon was one of the greatest in Greek history. It later featured in songs, plays and art.

The famous Greek playwright Aeschylus was at the battle, where his brother was killed. Aeschylus later said that he wanted to be remembered as one who fought at Marathon, not as a poet or a playwright. His play *The Persians* celebrated the famous victory:

*Woe, woe is me! Then has the iron storm,
That darkened from the realms of Asia,
poured In vain its arrowy shower on
sacred Greece.*

THE DEFENCE OF ATHENS

Persia may have lost the battle, but we had not yet lost the war and we still had a massive army aboard our ships. Our commanders gave the order to set sail for Athens, 40 km away.

BURN ATHENS!

The plan was to sail to the city and invade it before the Greek army could return home. By the time they got there, Athens would be a pile of smoking ruins.

Our commanders set sail for Athens as fast as possible. They knew the Athenians must be exhausted after the battle. There was no way they could get to Athens faster than our ships. Except ...

MARCH OF THE GREEKS

Within hours of us arriving in the seas off Athens, the Athenian army turned up. They had marched back at high speed, and somehow arrived before we could sack the city. Even worse, a load of Spartans had finally arrived to help. Our commanders have decided enough is enough. We are heading back to Asia. The invasion of Greece is off.

I fear what will happen next, now that the Greeks have beaten us in battle. Until Marathon, we have always been able to keep the Greeks back. Will that still be the case in the future?

HOW DO WE KNOW?

Legend says that a Greek messenger called Pheidippides ran 40 km back to Athens to deliver news of the Athenian victory at Marathon, then died.

This statue of Pheidippides shows him collapsing after delivering news of the Athenian victory at Marathon.

A medal from the 2005 Spartathlon race.

This legend is almost completely wrong. It mangles together two different stories told by Herodotus. The first describes Pheidippides, running 250 km to Sparta (and back), to call for help. The second tells of the whole army marching back to Athens, to stop a second Persian attack.

Today, the 250 km from Athens to Sparta has been turned into an annual Spartathlon race. Pheidippides is said to have run it in 36 hours, but the record holder is Greek ultra-runner Yiannis Kouros, with 20 hours and 25 minutes.

THANKS TO ATHENA

One thing the Athenians will be sure to do after their victory is offer gifts of thanks to Athena. She's the **patron** goddess of their city, which is named after her.

GIVING TO THE GODS

Like us Persians, the Greeks make offerings to the gods and goddesses. An offering is something precious. You give it to a god or goddess when you want help, or as thanks after things have turned out well. Offerings can be as small as a piece of bread, or as big as a cow.

WISDOM AND WAR

The Greeks believe that Athena is the favourite daughter of Zeus, chief of the gods. She has no mother – instead, she sprang fully formed from Zeus's head. She is the god of wisdom and war, among other things. General Miltiades owes her an especially good offering for his clever battle plan!

During the Panathenaia festival (see page 19) the people of Athens present a new robe to a statue of Athena.

PANATHENAIA

Every year in early summer the Athenians hold a festival for Athena; every four years they make it into a really big celebration. The festival is called the Panathenaia. There are athletics contests, chariot racing, music, dancing, **sacrifices** and a procession in Athena's honour.

CITIES AND GODS

It's not only Athens that has a patron god or goddess – every Greek city has one. Athena is one of the most popular: Sparta and Syracuse also have her. Apollo (god of light and music), Zeus, his wife Hera, the sea god Poseidon and Apollo's twin sister Artemis are all popular too.

HOW DO WE KNOW?

There is no one source for what we know about ancient Greek mythology. Our information comes from several writers, as well as from statues and carvings. A poet named Hesiod first wrote down the Greeks' stories of their gods and goddesses in about 700 BCE. The plays and poems of Greek writers such as Aeschylus (see page 15), Sophocles and Euripides also tell us about their mythology.

In the early 1800s this carving was taken from the Parthenon temple in Athens to London. It shows a scene from a procession celebrating Panathenaia.

THE GREEK NAVY

Now they think they can challenge the mighty Persia, the Athenians will start building up their navy. King Darius will NOT like the idea of hundreds of Greek warships patrolling the Mediterranean Sea!

SHIPS OF WAR

The Greeks have a variety of different warships. They are usually powered by a combination of sails and oars. The ships are long and narrow, with a deck for the fighting men to move along. The rowers sit below the deck, working long oars that stick out like a centipede's legs.

TOUGH TRIREMES

The most dangerous Greek ships are **triremes**. These warships are sometimes used for defence, but they are mainly used when a city is trying to expand its territory by taking on its neighbours. They carry soldiers and fight other ships. The rowers are free men, not **slaves** like in most other navies.

The front of the trireme is fitted with a large, metal-ended ram. Once the enemy ship is holed, it either sinks or has to be rowed ashore.

The Greeks are a dangerous enemy at sea – their triremes can sink transport ships by ramming them.

HOW DO WE KNOW?

In 489 BCE, within a year of the Battle of Marathon, the Athenians began to expand their navy. Records show that the Athenian fleet grew from 40 to 200 triremes in just nine years. The ships were paid for by the city, using money from a newly discovered silver mine. Once built, their upkeep was paid for by rich **citizens.**

In calm seas, the largest trireme could travel at 10 kph – faster than other large ships.

Triremes carry archers and 20 or more hoplites for attacking and capturing enemy ships.

GREEK SETTLERS

The Greeks caught us out at Marathon, but we Persians still have a massive empire. The worrying thing, though, is that the Greeks never stop trying to get more land.

FINDING FARMLAND

Most Greeks are farmers who live in the countryside. In many parts of Greece the soil is poor, so it is hard for farmers to make a living. That's one of the main reasons why so many Greeks sail off to look for new lands to live in. If they decide we Persians are weak now, it won't be long before the Greeks are nibbling away at our territory.

The Greeks are also expanding westward. They have been doing this for a long time: a hundred years ago, Greeks sailed off and started a new **colony** at Massalia.

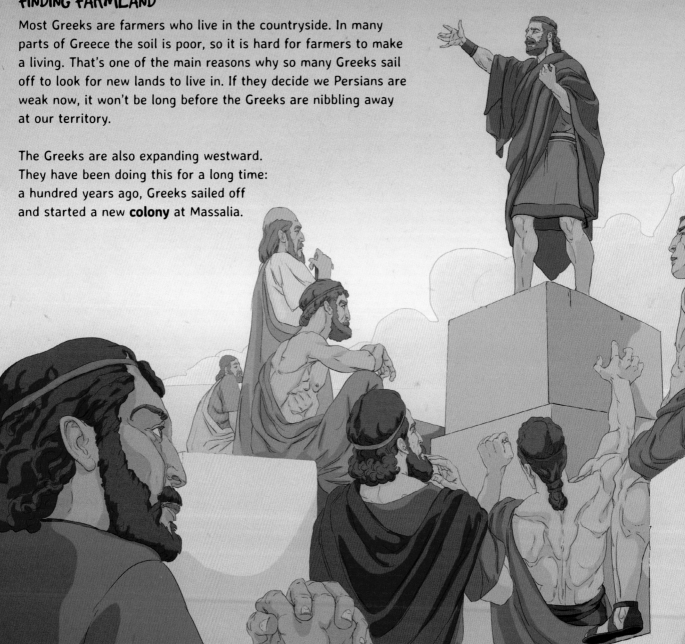

GREEK GOVERNMENT

Once the Greeks arrive somewhere and set up one of their colonies, they arrange the government. Greeks govern themselves in different ways.

Athens, for example, is a democracy. At least once a month, all male Athenian citizens who are 18 or more gather to make decisions. Sometimes there are thousands of them there, trying to agree on what to do. To a Persian, used to being told what to do by a single king, it sounds crazy!

The Spartans are also weird. They have kings, like us Persians – but they have two! Spartan kings work with a group of citizens. The kings can even be exiled if they become unpopular.

HOW DO WE KNOW?

One of the most successful Greek settlements was the city of Massalia in France. The Massalian Greeks traded wine, olive oil and precious metals up the Rhone river and into the heart of Europe. Massalia was such a successful colony that it eventually became independent. Today the city is known as Marseille.

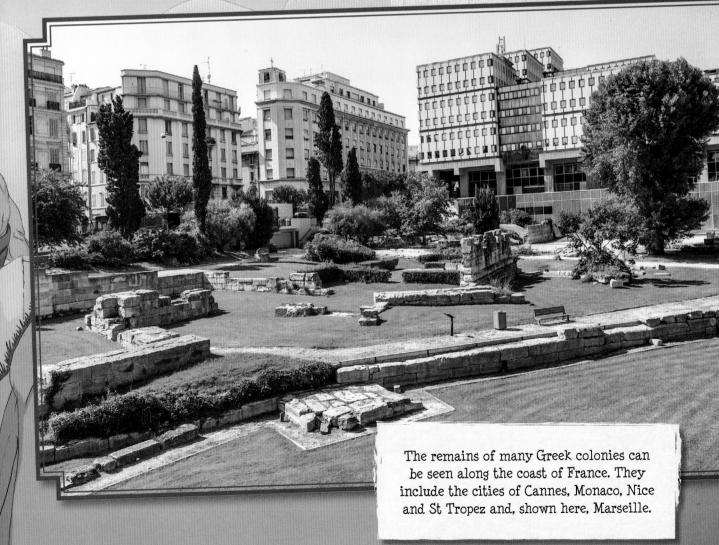

The remains of many Greek colonies can be seen along the coast of France. They include the cities of Cannes, Monaco, Nice and St Tropez and, shown here, Marseille.

GREEK ENTERTAINMENT

Of course, even a loyal Persian like me has to admit that the Greeks aren't all bad. If they do invade your area, they bring one or two good things with them.

GREEK THEATRE

For a start, Greeks LOVE theatre. Every Greek town has a theatre. It is usually a bowl-shaped space out on a hillside, with hard stone seats.

There are only three kinds of play: comedies, tragedies and satyrs. Satyrs are rude half-man, half-goat creatures, and satyr plays are rude, too.

If people like a play, they cheer and stamp their feet. If they don't like it, they shout abuse and even throw food at the actors. It can get a bit rough, so the staff at the theatre have big sticks for keeping the audience in line.

THE OLYMPICS

If there is anything the Greeks love even more than theatre, it is the Olympics. This is a huge sports festival in honour of the god Zeus, held every four years. There are all kinds of events: chariot racing, running, throwing and fighting. The scariest is pankration, a combat sport where almost anything is allowed ... except biting or poking people's eyes.

The games are so important that wars are stopped a month before to let Greek athletes travel to the games safely. This is called the 'Sacred Truce'. Win at the Olympics and you are set up for life. Your city will be so proud that you will probably never have to work again!

HOW DO WE KNOW?

Archaeologists have uncovered many Greek theatres. They have also investigated the site of the Olympics.

Pottery and carvings from the Greek world show us Olympic athletes in action, while writings tell us about how the Greeks had fun. For example, an **inscription** from ancient Athens tells us of one reward for Olympic winners: a free meal at the town hall every day for the rest of your life!

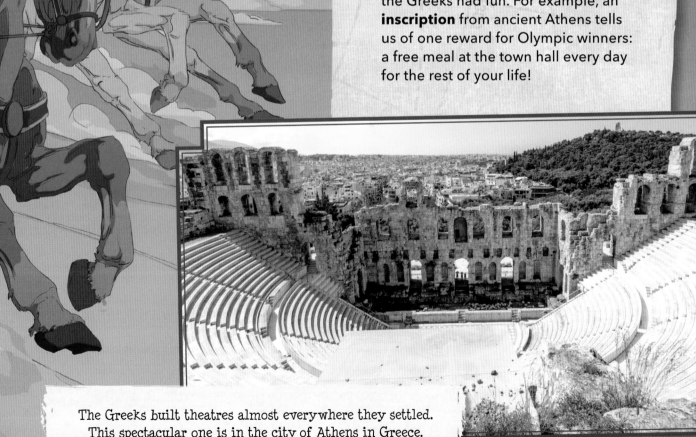

The Greeks built theatres almost everywhere they settled. This spectacular one is in the city of Athens in Greece.

CRIME AND PUNISHMENT

Of course, theatres and games are not the only things the Greeks will bring to your neighbourhood. Step out of line and you'll discover a range of punishments that starts with humiliation and ends at strangulation.

GUILTY OR NOT GUILTY?

What happens to someone accused of a crime depends on which Greeks you're invaded by, but the Athenians are fairly typical.

For a serious crime, people appear in front of a jury of hundreds (sometimes thousands). The two sides give their versions of events, then the jury votes: 'guilty', or 'not guilty'. Whichever gets the most votes – even if it's just one more or fewer – that's the result.

Athenians often let criminals escape even if the verdict is 'guilty'. No one goes after them – they just can't ever come back.

PUNISHMENTS

The actual punishments get more serious depending on your crime:

- A fine: for small crimes, a fine may be all you suffer (which is serious for poor people, who stay in prison until they can pay)
- Being put in the **stocks** and humiliated by having people jeer at you, throw rotten fruit, etc
- If you are a slave, being beaten, whipped or imprisoned
- Losing the right to take part in politics
- Exile, which can be temporary or permanent
- Having your house pulled down and all your belongings taken away
- Execution, usually by being strangled – though if you are rich or have rich friends, you will probably be allowed to poison yourself by drinking **hemlock** instead.

This statue of Plato is outside the modern-day Academy in Athens, one of Greece's most important research centres.

HOW DO WE KNOW?

Several writers from ancient Greece have told us about laws, crimes and punishments. They include the famous Greek thinker Plato (c.427–347 BCE). We know a lot about Plato because almost everything he wrote has survived.

In Athens, Plato founded the Academy. This was a place where people could come to study **philosophy** and mathematics, among other things. It was a kind of university – the first one in Europe.

THE RISE AND FALL OF ANCIENT GREECE

After the victory at Marathon in 490 BCE, Greek power continued to grow. The Greeks began to push against the Persian Empire to the east, and expanded their colonies to the west.

The second Persian invasion

Ten years after Marathon, Xerxes, the new king of Persia, attempted a second invasion of Greece. A small, Spartan-led force held back Xerxes's army of 100,000 men at a place called Thermopylae. At almost the same time, the Athenian navy defeated a Persian fleet of about 500 ships. Fearing he would be trapped in Greece, Xerxes returned to Asia.

The Peloponnesian War and rise of Macedonia

Having fought off Persia, Sparta and Athens soon became rivals. From 431–404 BCE, Greece was divided by the Peloponnesian War between the two powerful city states. Sparta won, but eventually its power began to fail.

By 338 BCE, there was a new power in Greece: a northern kingdom called Macedonia. Led by their king, Philip II, the Macedonians took control of territory all the way to Byzantium. This is now Istanbul, the city where Europe ends and Asia begins.

The memorial to the Spartan warriors at Thermopylae, Greece.

Alexander the Great

When Philip II was assassinated in 336 BCE, his son Alexander became king. Alexander led his armies into Persia, where they won victory after victory. The young king became known as Alexander the Great. Greek power spread east to the borders of India, and south to Egypt. By the time Alexander died of a fever in 323 BCE, Greek culture and ideas had spread throughout the eastern Mediterranean.

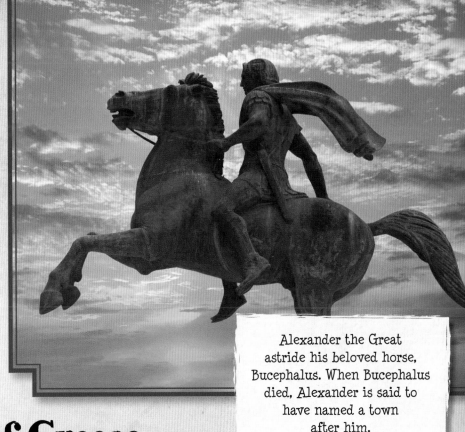

Alexander the Great astride his beloved horse, Bucephalus. When Bucephalus died, Alexander is said to have named a town after him.

The decline of Greece

By around 200 BCE, Rome was becoming increasingly powerful and Greece's influence began to fade. In 31 BCE the Roman emperor Octavian defeated the Egyptians at the Battle of Actium. Historians judge that this was the moment when ideas from Rome, not Greece, became the most important in Europe.

The ancient Greek Olympics inspired our modern-day Olympic Games. The five Olympic rings represent Africa, Asia, the Americas, Australia and Europe.

What did the Greeks do for us?

The influence of the ancient Greeks is still felt around the world today:

- Democracy, the system of government in which citizens get a say in how their country is run, was a Greek idea
- Our art and **architecture** are both influenced by Greek style
- Many popular sports and sports events are based on Greek ideas
- New ideas in science, mathematics and history all developed in Greece.

GLOSSARY

alliance agreement between two people or organisations that they will support each other

archaeology study of actual objects from ancient times

architecture design of buildings

border edge; for a country, its border is the edge of its territory

cavalry the soldiers in an army who fight on horseback

citizen legal member of a country or place, who has the right to vote in elections

city-state a state made up of a city and the land that it controls

colony area controlled and settled by people from another country

exile send to live in a foreign country and never allow to return

hemlock a poisonous plant

inscription writing that has been cut into stone or rock

javelin spear designed for throwing

mercenary solider who fights for anyone who will pay, rather than only for their own country

Mithra Persian god of war

mythology The myths or stories associated with a particular culture

neutral not on one side or the other of an argument

patron person, usually someone powerful, who supports and helps others

philosophy study of ideas, for example ideas about right and wrong, what we know and do not know, or what makes something valuable

revolt resist or fight against the authorities

rival person or organisation that competes with another for the same thing

sack destroy, after taking away everything valuable

sacrifice killing an animal in honour of a god

slave person whose freedom is taken away, who is forced to work for nothing

source place where we get information

stocks device for holding people in one place, usually by clamping their ankles, wrists and/or neck

strategy plan of actions leading to a specific aim

trireme warship powered by three rows of oars, as well as a sail or sails

volley lots of arrows, bullets or other items all launched at the enemy at once

---

Great Greek insults

The Greeks were excellent at insults, as this exchange between the politicians Demosthenes and Phocion shows:

> Demosthenes: *The Athenians will kill you, Phocion, if they go crazy.*

> Phocion: *But they will kill you if they come to their senses.*

Here are a couple of names to use when you feel like insulting someone, ancient-Greek style:

Morosoph! (An educated person who is nonetheless a fool.)

Troglodytus! (Primitive person who lives in a cave.)

Timeline of Ancient Greece

2200 BCE	1450 BCE	1100–800 BCE	800–700 BCE	776 BCE	508 BCE	499–449 BCE	490 BCE
Minoan civilisation flourishes on Crete.	The Mycenaean civilisation flourishes in Greece.	Dark Age in Greece.	Homer writes *The Odyssey*.	The first Olympic Games take place.	Democracy begins in Athens.	The Greco-Persian Wars.	The Battle of Marathon between the Athenians and the Persians.

FINDING OUT MORE

Places to visit

There are many places you can visit to see objects from ancient Greece. Here are just a few:

The British Museum
Great Russell St
Bloomsbury
London WC1B 3DG

At the British Museum you can see many objects from ancient Greece, including the famous Parthenon Sculptures (sometimes called the Elgin Marbles).

There is more information about the museum on its website, www.britishmuseum.org.

The section for teachers and schoolchildren is here: www.britishmuseum.org/learn/schools/ages-7-11/ancient-greece.

The Museum of Classical Archaeology in Cambridge (www.classics.cam.ac.uk/museum) is filled with over 400 plaster-cast copies of ancient Greek and Roman sculptures. One of the highlights is the statue of a girl from ancient Greece painted in its original bright colours. Also in Cambridge, the Fitzwilliam Museum (www.fitzmuseum.cam.ac.uk) has a range of objects from ancient Greece.

The Acropolis Museum in Greece celebrates ancient Greek culture and contains some amazing archaeological discoveries. Find out more at: www.theacropolismuseum.gr.

Books to read

Alexander the Great and the Ancient Greeks David Gill (Franklin Watts, 2016)

The life and times of probably the most famous person in the whole of Greek history: Alexander the Great, a man so powerful he could name a city after his favourite horse. (The horse was called Bucephalus, the city – which was in Pakistan – Bucephala.)

Stars of Mythology: The Greeks Nancy Dickmann (Franklin Watts, 2017)

Introducing the gods, goddesses, monsters and heroes of Greek myths – in their own words (possibly …)

The Best (And Worst) Jobs in Ancient Greece Clive Gifford (Wayland, 2017)

Being a priest was a top job in ancient Greece, but you couldn't become one if you were in debt or were a deserter. Maybe you'd rather be a doctor? You would have to promise not to poison your patients. This book is a great introduction to the kinds of jobs people did in ancient Greece.

A Visitor's Guide to Ancient Greece Lesley Sims (Usborne, 2014)

Anyone considering a time-travel holiday to ancient Greece will need a copy of this book. It tells about the festivals, tourist attractions, fashions and customs of the Greeks, allowing you to plan a fun-packed trip to the ancient world.

---

480 BCE
The Battle of Thermopylae and other battles during which the Greeks are eventually victorious over the Persian Empire.

431–404 BCE
The Second Peloponnesian Wars are fought between Athens, Sparta and other city-states.

359 BCE
King Philip II is king of Macedonia and Greece.

336–323 BCE
King Alexander the Great expands the Greek Empire.

229 BCE
The ancient Romans start meddling in Greece's affairs.

146 BCE
Greece and Macedonia become part of the Roman Empire.

INDEX

Academy, Athens 27
Aeschylus 15, 19
archaeology 5, 9, 11, 25
archers 9, 11–14, 20
armies
      Athenians 6, 8, 10–17, 20
      Persian 6–9, 11–17
      Spartan 8, 17
armour 10–12, 14
Athena 18–19
Athens/Athenians 4, 6–7, 9,
    12–21, 23, 25–28
athletics 19, 25

Battle of Actium 29
Battle of Marathon 14–15, 21,
    22, 28
Bucephalus 29

Carneia 9
Carthagians 4
cavalry 12–14
colonies, Greek 22–23, 28
Crete 4
crimes 26–27

Dark Age 5
democracy 23, 29

Emperor Octavian 29
entertainment 24–25

farmers 22
festivals 9, 18–19

gods and goddesses 14, 18–19, 25
government 23, 29

Hellas 4
Herodotus 7, 9, 13, 17
Hesiod 19–20
Homer 5
hoplites 10–15, 20
horse, wooden 5

Ionian Revolt 6–7, 10

King Alexander the Great 29
King Darius 6–7, 9, 20
King Philip II 28–29
King Xerxes 28
Kouros, Yiannis 17

laws 26–27

Macedonia 4, 28–29
Marathon 7, 9, 12, 14–15, 17, 22,
    28
Massalia 22–23
mercenaries 12
Miltiades 15, 18
Minoans 4
Mithra 14
Mycenaeans 5
myths, Greek 19, 28

navy, Greek 20–21, 28

Olympic Games 25, 26, 29

Panathenaia 18–19
Parthenon 19
Peloponnesian War 28
Persian Empire/Persians 4–18,
    20–23, 28–29
phalanxes 11, 12, 14
Pheidippides 17
Plataeans 9
Plato 27
plays 5, 15, 19, 24
pottery 4, 11, 25
punishments 26–27

religion 5, 9, 14, 18–19
Romans 4, 29

Sardis 6
settlers, Greek 22–23
ships 4, 14–16, 20–21, 28

Sparta/Spartans 4, 8–9, 17, 19,
    23, 28
Spartathlon race 17
sport 25, 29
statues 4, 7, 17–19, 27
Syracuse 19

tactics, fighting 11
temples 5, 9, 19
The *Histories* 7
The *Odyssey* 5
The Persians 15
theatres 24–25, 26
Thermopylae 28
triremes 20–21
Troy 5

warships 20–21
weapons 5, 9, 10–14
wreaths, olive 5
writers 5, 7, 9, 13, 15, 19–20, 25,
    27